Finding XYZ : The Great Alphabet Hunt

Paula Curtis Taylorson

illustrated by Zaida Montes

Finding XYZ : The Great Alphabet Hunt

This is a work of fiction.

Text and Illustrations copyrighted

by Paula Curtis Taylorson ©2021

Library of Congress Control Number: 2021905045

All rights reserved. No part of this book may be reproduced, transmitted, or stored in an information retrieval system in any form or by any means, graphic, electronic, or mechanical without prior written permission from the author.

Printed in the United States of America

A 2 Z Press LLC

PO Box 582

Deleon Springs, FL 32130

bestlittleonlinebookstore.com

sizemore3630@aol.com

440-241-3126

ISBN: 978-1-954191-25-9

Dedication

Thank you to those who read to me and those who listened to me read.

This Book Belongs To:

_____

Xavier is a **zoo**keeper from Croatia,
he works at the **Zagreb Zoo**,
Looking after all of the **X, Y and Zs**,
is a difficult job to do!

He starts work ever so early,
zooming around with feed in his cart,

Zig-zagging between the animals as he checks them off on his chart.

His first stop is at the **zebras**,
to feed **Yuri**, **Yosef** and **Yazzy**,

Two have the usual **zany** stripes,
while the other is a little bit jazzy!

Xavier gives them fresh **zucchini** and **zesty** lemonade to drink,

Yosef and Yuri gobbled theirs up, but Yazzy shares his with a mink.

Now it's off to see **Xena** the **yak**, who lives on a **yacht** on the lake,

Two **Yorkshire** terriers dig up the dinosaur bones of a **Yandusaurus**,

Chimpanzees play trapeze on **zip-wire**, while **yabbies** are practicing **yoga**,

The zebra finches fly in a formation, that spells out the word zabaglione, (zab-ah-glee-oh-knee)

Zoe, the elephant from **Zimbabwe**, needs an **xray** of her swollen leg,

She was knitting a **Zulu** skirt with **yarn**, and slipped on the **yolk** of an egg!

She said, "You're in need of some **Zen** treatment, at the **Yishun** hospital way over in Singapore!"

In the gift shop, **Yvette** sells **Yuzu** ice cream topped with sweet **yellow** fruit,

Some **youngsters** yell "**Yahoo!**" as they wave to **Xavier** inside the lion compound,

And **Zara**, a hippo from a river in **Zambezi**, dreams of riding a merry-go-round!

A **Zumbador,** a South American hummingbird, hums tunes on his **zappy** cell phone,

And a **zeppelin** flies **yonder** on its way to New **York**, carrying spices from old **Zanzibar!**

Some first-**years** are on their way to a Halloween party, they are dressed up as **zombies** for fun,

Where they **zap** around scaring **zillions** there, then **zip** down to the penguin ski run!

There's a fountain in the **zoo** that is lucky,
if **you** throw coins in **your** wishes come true,

The End

My Very Own 'XY and Z' Words:

Glossary

Page 1. **Xavier** : a boy's name
Zookeeper : a person who cares for the animals in a zoo
Zagreb : a city in and the capital of Croatia, in the northwestern part
Zoo : a park-like area in which live animals are kept in cages or large enclosures for public exhibition
X, Y and Zs : letters

Page 2. **Zooming** : to move quickly or suddenly with a loud humming or buzzing sound

Page 3. **Zig zagging** : a line, course, or progression characterized by sharp turns first to one side and then to the other

Page 4. **Zebras** : an animal from Africa that resembles a horse but has a characteristic pattern of black or dark-brown stripes on a whitish background, all zebra species are threatened or endangered
Yuri : the name of the zebra here
Yosef : the name of the zebra here
Yazzy : the name of the zebra here

Pag 5. **Zany** : comical; clownish.

Page 6. **Xavier** : the boy's name
Zucchini : a vegetable
Zesty : flavorful for this book, energetic

Page 7. **Yosef** : the name of the zebra here
Yuri : the name of the zebra here
Yazzy : the name of the zebra here

Page 8. **Xena** : a girl's name
Yak : a large, stocky, shaggy-haired wild ox that has long, curved horns, they are endangered
Yacht : a large boat

Page 9. **Yoghurt** : a tart, custardlike food made from milk curdled by the action of bacterial cultures, sometimes sweetened or flavored.
Zingers : cake deserts, sweets
Yummy : very good tasting

Page 10. **Yorkshire** terrier : a dog
Yandusaurus : Yandusaurus is a genus of herbivorous basal neornithischian dinosaur from the Bathonian age of China

Page 11. **Zach** : a boy's name
Young : not old
Zoologist : the science or branch of biology dealing with animals
Zephyrosaurus : meaning "westward wind lizard") is a genus of orodromine ornithischian dinosaur

Page 12. **Zip wire** : a thin wire to balance on
Yabbies : a crayfish from Australia
Yoga : any of the methods or disciplines prescribed, especially a series of postures and breathing exercises used to achieve control of the body and mind, tranquility

Page 13. **Zonkey** : half zebra, half donkey
Zebra : an animal from Africa that resembles a horse but has a characteristic pattern of black or dark-brown stripes on a whitish background, all zebra species are threatened or endangered

Page 14. **Zebra finches** : small birds
Zabaglione : a foamy, custard-like mixture of egg yolks, sugar, and Marsala wine, usually served hot or chilled as a dessert

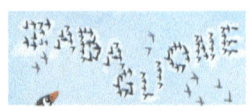

Page 15. **Yawning** : to open the mouth wide with a long, deep breath and sighing or heavy exhalation, as from drowsiness or boredom
Zorilla : a skunk-like African mammal with a long black-and-white coat

Page 16. **Zoe** : a girl's name
Zimbabwe : a country on the continent of Africa
Xray : an image to see the bones of an animal or person

Page 17. **Zulu skirt** : clothing
Yarn : thread made of natural or synthetic fibers and used for knitting and weaving.
Yolk : the yellow part of an egg, as distinguished from the white

Page 18. **Vet/veterinarian** : doctor for animals
New **Zealand** : a country
Yikes : an exclamation of surprise or alarm

Page 19. **Zen** treatment : Chinese treatment for care
Yishun : Yishun, formerly known as Nee Soon, is a residential town located in the northeastern corner of the North Region of Singapore, a country

Page 20. **Yvette** : a girl's name
Yuzu : a citrus fruit about the size of a golf ball, a combination of a citrus friut and a mandarin, which grows on tall trees in Japan and has a strong sour flavour. Its rind and juice are a popular ingredient in Japanese cookery
Yellow : a color

Page 21. **Yoyos** : a toy on a string
Yucca : a plant
Xanadu : , a large shopping precinct and entertainment centre in Spain - a metaphor for opulence or an idyllic place, make believe place

Page 22. **Youngsters** : young children, not old
Yell : speak loudly
"**Yahoo**!" : an exclamation used to express joy, excitement

Page 23. **Zara** : a girl's name
Zambezi : a country in Africa

Page 24. **Zumbador** : a South American hummingbird

Page 25. **Yodel's** : to sing with frequent changes from the ordinary voice to falsetto and back again, in the manner of Swiss and Tyrolean mountaineers
Yeti : the Abominable Snowman in Himalayan folklore, is an ape-like creature said to inhabit the Himalayan mountain range in Asia
Zealously : happy, energetic
Xylophone : a musical instrument consisting of a graduated series of wooden bars, usually sounded by striking with small wooden hammers

Page 26. **Zebrafish** : zebrafish is a freshwater that lives in South Asia, a popular aquarium fish
Zumba : a fitness program of dance and exercise Done to Latin American music
Year-round : all during the year
Xander : a famous musician
zither guitar : a musical instrument with a sound-box with two sets of strings

Page 27. **Zeppelin** : a large balloon that flies
Yonder: somewhere far away
New **York** : a city in America
Zanzibar : an island off the east coast of Africa

Page 28. First-**years** : first-grade students
Zombies : a person whose behavior or responses are stiff, listless, or seemingly rote, an eccentric or peculiar person

Page 29. **Zap** : to touch quickly
Zillions : an extremely large, indeterminate number
Zip : move quickly

Page 30. **Zoo** : a park-like area in which live animals are kept in cages or large enclosures for public exhibition

Page 31. **Zloty** : a nickel coin and monetary unit of Poland, equal to 100 groszy
Yen : an aluminum coin and monetary unit of Japan equal to 100 sen or 1000 rin,
a former silver coin of Japan

Page 33. **Yippee** : an exclamation used to express joy, exultation, or the like
You've : a contracted word for you have

Paula Curtis-Taylorson Lives in Marston Mortaine, England. She is a full-time secondary school teacher of English and English Literature. She was amongst the first of the initial students to graduate from the Uk's first BA (Hons) Creative Writing Program at the University of Bedfordshire.

Her first love is poetry and rhyme and she works hard to inspire and teach appreciation of the subject to all age groups. Many of her students have gone on to be successful writers.

www.ingramcontent.com/pod-product-compliance
Lightning Source LLC
Chambersburg PA
CBHW061105070526
44579CB00011B/142